POO AT THE ZOO

by

John Wood

Minneapolis, Minnesota

Credits:
All images are courtesy of Shutterstock.com, unless otherwise specified. With thanks to Getty Images, Thinkstock Photo, and iStockphoto.

Front Cover – Sensvector, Roman Samokhin. Title typeface used throughout – PremiumVector. Vector flies – Top Vector Studio. 2 – Tom Reichner. 4–5 – DimaSid, Erwin Bosman, Granate Art, SurfsUp. 6–7 – Eric Isselee, Passakorn Umpornmaha, Pegasene. 8–9 – Ondrej Prosicky, OSTILL is Franck Camhi, tanyabosyk, NadiiaKushnyrenko. 10–11 – Peter Mullineux, Eric Isselee, GoodFocused, Irina oxilixo Danilova. 12–13 – Stu Porter, Alta Oosthuizen, Alfmaler. 14–15 – Krakenimages.com, Eric Isselee, Linn Currie, Colorcocktail. 16–17 – Aaron Welch, Kimmo Hagman, jehsomwang, pikepicture. 18–19 – BearFotos, OSDG, Jody, lady-luck. 20–21 – Daria Shuiskova, Jiri Viehmann, WinWin artlab, Designer things. 22–23 – Alessandro Tortora, Martin Mecnarowski, MVshop, Colorcocktail.

Bearport Publishing Company Product Development Team
Publisher: Jen Jenson; Director of Product Development: Spencer Brinker; Managing Editor: Allison Juda; Editor: Cole Nelson; Associate Editor: Naomi Reich; Associate Editor: Tiana Tran; Art Director: Colin O'Dea; Designer: Kim Jones; Designer: Kayla Eggert; Product Development Specialist: Owen Hamlin

Library of Congress Cataloging-in-Publication Data is available at www.loc.gov or upon request from the publisher.

ISBN: 979-8-89232-752-7 (hardcover)
ISBN: 979-8-89232-802-9 (paperback)
ISBN: 979-8-89232-839-5 (ebook)

For more information, write to Bearport Publishing, 5357 Penn Avenue South, Minneapolis, MN 55419.

CONTENTS

ALL ABOUT POO

Zoos are full of poo! But do you know whose poo is whose? Watch your step, and let's find out whose poo is at the zoo.

Poo is important to zookeepers. It tells them about the health of animals.

On the next pages, you will see some poo at the zoo. Learn about the poo, and choose which animal you think it belongs to. Then, turn the page to see if you were right!

Don't touch any poo you find at the zoo. Poo has lots of nasty things in it!

WET AND SLOPPY

Look at this green poo. Whose poo is it?

Whose poo could this be? Choose which of these three animals you think did it.

Green poo from a red panda? Surely not....

Macaw

This poo has splattered. The animal must have been very high up.

There is a lot of this poo around. The animal probably lives in a group.

WHOSE POO WAS IT?

Macaws eat mostly fruits, seeds, and **insects**. They have curved **beaks** and scaly tongues that have a bone inside. The birds use their beaks and tongues to break open seeds.

Macaws poo and pee from the same part of their bodies. The colorless liquid part and the stringy white part of their droppings is pee. The solid green part is the poo.

Macaw poo is not always green. Macaws that eat red foods will have reddish poo.

Some wild macaws eat bits of clay. This helps them **digest** foods that would otherwise make them sick.

BIG, STINKY, AND FULL OF FUR

This is one of the biggest poos at the zoo! Whose is it?

There are bits of fur and bone in the poo. This animal must eat other animals.

The poo is huge! The animal that made it must be big, too.

Whose poo could this be? Choose which of these three animals you think did it.
Lion
This poo is hard and mostly dry. It's been here for a while.
That poo is almost as big as me!
Meerkat
This poo is out in the open. The animal probably wants it to be seen.
Iguana

WHOSE POO WAS IT?

Lions eat other animals, such as zebras, buffalo, and **rodents**. Bones and fur are hard to digest. So, they often come out in a lion's poo.

In the wild, lions usually don't cover their poo like smaller cats do. They leave it in the open to help mark their **territory**.

LOADS OF GRASS AND SEEDS

Someone had a big lunch! There is so much poo here, but whose is it?

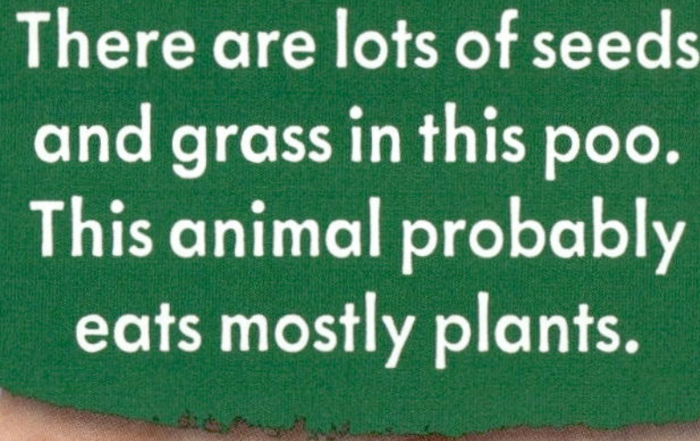

There are lots of seeds and grass in this poo. This animal probably eats mostly plants.

This is a big pile of poo. The animal must be big, too.

Whose poo could it be? Choose which of these three animals you think did it.
Rhinoceros
This poo is out in the open. There are other piles nearby, too.
Ostrich
Lynx
Plants and grass? No thanks! Where's the meat?

WHOSE POO WAS IT?

It was the **rhinoceros's POO!**

I don't even remember eating those seeds!

Rhinoceroses eat plants. The seeds from these plants come out in their poo and eventually begin to grow. So, rhinos help plants spread when they poo.

Rhinos use their poo to **communicate**, too. Many rhinos drop their poo in the same spot. The different smells in all this poo tells rhinos about one another.

Rhinos can tell the age and health of another rhino by smelling its poo.

PLENTY OF PELLETS

There is another poo. Who left this behind?

This poo is made up of tiny, round **pellets**. The pellets are close together in piles.

There are lots of piles of this poo. Maybe this was made by a large animal.

Whose poo could it be? Choose which of these three animals you think did it.

These droppings are dark and not too smelly.

Do you think my poo would look like that?

Flamingo

The pellets are smooth and dry.

Gorilla

WHOSE POO WAS IT?

It was the **reindeer's POO!**

It was mine! Another helping of moss for me, please!

Reindeer eat grass, moss, and leaves. Since the food they eat is pretty dry, their poo is dry, too.

Reindeer often chew their food twice. They throw up the food they ate into their mouths and chew it again. This makes the food easier to digest. It's also why their poo is smooth.

In the winter, wild reindeer may travel more than 1,000 miles (1,600 km) to find food.

Reindeer poo a lot! They may poo up to 15 times a day.

BONUS POO!

POO IS ON THE MENU

Lemurs eat their own poo! Sometimes, lemurs eat the poo of other animals, too. *Yuck!*

Animals eat poo for lots of reasons. There may still be **nutrients** in the poo. It can also have water in it. Animals in dry places need this water.

GLOSSARY

beaks hard mouthparts used to eat

communicate to pass information between two or more things

digest to break down food into things that can be used by the body

insects animals that have six legs, three body parts, and a hard covering

liquid a thing that flows, such as water

nutrients natural substances that plants and animals need to grow and stay healthy

pellets small, hard balls of poop or undigested food

rodents animals, such as rats and mice, that have four feet and long front teeth

territory the area where an animal lives and finds its food

INDEX